HOPES AND DREAMS

POEMS BY
DAISAKU IKEDA

Translated by Robert Epp

International Standard Book Number: 0-915678-06-3
Library of Congress Catalog Card Number: 75-458-42
The World Tribune Press, Santa Monica, CA. 90406

Printed in the United States of America

Contents

TRANSLATOR'S NOTE 7

PREFACE 11

POEMS

Up from the Soil 16
The Crisp Day We Parted 18
Scattered Blossoms 20
Pampas Grass 24
Mt. Fuji and I 28
Snow 31
Night 34
The Sea in May 36
Autumn Flame 38
Time 40
Title 44
The Life of a Literary Giant 45
Genius 48
Travelers 50
Dreams 52
Treasures 54
Believer 55
Angels of Peace 56
My Friends Behind the Scenes 60
Hope 62
Young Boys 66

NOTES ON THE POEMS 73

ABOUT THE AUTHOR 77

Translator's Note

Few would disagree with Tsurayuki's statement in the Preface to his tenth-century verse collection, the *Kokinshu,* that poetry "has its root in the human heart." Or with Lady Murasaki, who assures us in her eleventh-century *Tale of Genji* that a man writes because he has been so profoundly moved he cannot keep his feelings "shut up in his heart." Over the centuries, Japanese prose and poetry have honored feeling over intellect. Daisaku Ikeda himself has written: "Verse . . . allows succinct expression of what one feels." It is only when we look at the content of his verse and consider the driving spirit behind it that we discover how it differs from classical poetry on the one hand and modern on the other.

Classical Japanese poems celebrate intensely personal experiences. But they are concerned primarily with love or nature, with the emptiness of longing, the evanescence of life and beauty or with loneliness and the like: "Aching for her / I spend this endless day / Deep in thought"; "If I hear of your longing / I'll come back to you"; "The sheen of the petals / Has faded away"; "No one can know / Where spring has gone." These images reveal the pastimes of a leisured class dedicated to cultivating an exquisite mood of sadness and loss, mastering a corpus of traditional poems so they could allude to it in their own verse, and honing sensitivities to natural phenomena and seasonal change.

Daisaku Ikeda's verse deals similarly with intensely personal experiences. But both the nature of these experiences and the spirit that shapes his expressions differ markedly from the classical Muse. He writes as a busy workingman to busy workingmen, even to girls and boys. His tone is one of joy and victory, not of sadness and loss. His primary metaphors (infused less with shadows than with sunlight) deal with hope, the struggle to challenge and improve oneself, the search for principles to guide one's life, the attitudes needed to overcome difficulties. In short, Mr. Ikeda's is a poetry of commitment rather than of aesthetic sensibility and melancholy gentility. An architect of meaningfulness in life, he writes to enlighten and uplift; he is totally unconcerned with proving to other poets that he is a poet.

Modern verse, far more personal than the classical variety, centers on the individual poet's psyche. It is no exaggeration to claim that the driving spirit behind modern poetry lies close to Walt Whitman's ideal to "celebrate myself, and sing myself." That is why modern poets are so painfully self-conscious about their sense of alienation. They believe themselves a step ahead of their age or, at least, totally out of step with it: "When I clench my fists / And pound the shell of this prison world / My knuckles turn to blood"; "I climb that sad hill where sun sets / And roam aimlessly over the clifftop / But I shall never know where home is / Nor ever feel that I belong." Such egocentricity is incapable of displaying much interest in the anxieties and dreams of the common man. But then it is far easier to explore the tortured psyche, the darker aspects of the human situation, than to celebrate the sunlight.

This is to claim that the driving spirit – the "heart" or the *kokoro* – behind Mr. Ikeda's poetry is unique. It differs considerably from the *kokoro* of traditional Japanese verse and of most modern poetry as well. Indeed, if it were not for the transparency and immediacy of his tone of committed concern, some of Mr. Ikeda's poetry might be quite difficult indeed for the average reader.

The verbal texture of the language through which he expresses his *kokoro* is often complex. His verse contains a sufficiently large number of difficult compounds, illusive grammatical structures and in-group terminology to slow down readers with only a modest Japanese education. On the surface, these pitfalls seem to resemble the contradiction evident in Whitman's verse, where an avant garde rhetoric failed to communicate to the very contemporaries the poet so passionately claimed to be addressing; he was also probably a bit too interested in celebrating himself to appeal immediately to the average man of his day.

Beyond the surface, however, it is evident that the meaning of textual complexities in Ikeda differs radically from that in Whitman. For one thing, Daisaku Ikeda's conspicuous concern for people manifests itself even in his most opaque expression. For another, readers can use knowledge of his *kokoro* as a key to any difficulties they encounter. In contrast to Whitman, moreover, there is a genuine bond between poet and audience, a dialogue enhanced by the reader's dynamic sympathy with the poet's basic philosophy of life as well as by deep respect for a man who writes poetry for them. Identification with the poet and his values functions to encourage an output of effort to wade through textual perplexities which the casual reader of Whitman's works would never dream of. Even with regard to the level of the language used to uplift, then, Ikeda

Sensei tacitly challenges his people to try a bit harder and reach a bit higher in order to improve themselves.

The process of translation is equally indebted to this lucid *kokoro*. Without some grasp of the driving spirit behind Ikeda's verse, in fact, an outsider might confront grave problems in trying to render it into English. Strange to say, many knots in the verbal texture disappear in translation. One reason is that Japanese usually becomes clearer when converted into English, a language which demands expression of the subjects and referents so frequently and so lovingly avoided by the Japanese writer. The Japanese reader really seems to prefer a somewhat less lucid style than most English readers can tolerate, and he rarely values clarity as a virtue in a writer. Another reason is that a concerted effort has been made to render problematic passages into English that is simpler, though perhaps less interesting, than the original.

It goes without saying that very little in this volume could have been translated without help from others. I am especially grateful for the unfailing assistance of *World Tribune* staff members, who have also provided notes to supplement a number of the poems. And I appreciate help from Dr. Akira Nakamura in the work's initial stages. Even after an opaque passage has been explained, however, one must still convert an understanding of the text into convincing and natural English. Obviously the translator alone assumes responsibility for the stilted expressions, defective solutions and misleading interpretations that remain.

A negative, pessimistic and neurotic attitude toward life is the perfect antithesis of Mr. Ikeda's positive, optimistic and wholesome approach to writing. He can admire a poet like Whitman whose verse he says "powerfully exalts the cries of the individual." But his admiration is probably rooted less in Whitman's stress on individualism itself than in the unabashed glorification of common people: "the carpenter singing his (song) as he measures his plank or beam," or the "delicious singing of the mother, or of the young wife at work, or of the girl sewing and washing" (from "I Hear America Singing"). These are, after all, the basic concerns of Daisaku Ikeda, too. As the verse in this collection illustrates, the feelings which move him to write stem almost entirely from commitment to others. He wants people to grasp those positive attitudes which lend meaning to life and offer the fresh hope that anyone who tries can experience the sheer joy of *being*.

If it is true that the act of translation does unpardonable damage to prose, certainly it does incalculable violence to poetry. What a translator hopes is that the spirit of the original will survive his efforts. If President Ikeda's *kokoro* survives in these English versions of his poems, they will not betray the author's hope to implant the seeds of his thought in every reader's heart.

ROBERT EPP

November 1975

University of California,
Los Angeles

Preface

Needless to say, I am not a poet. Nor have I ever spent so much as a single moment studying how to write verse. But ever since I was a boy I have been fond of poetry, finding particular enjoyment in reading Walt Whitman in translation or Japanese poets like Doi Bansui (1871-1952). From time to time, in an attempt to express some personal inspiration or idea, I have produced my own brand of poetry.

My fondness for verse stems from the fact that it allows succinct expression of what one feels about something. Verse is indeed quite well suited to my own temperament. My adolescence was spent during the pitiful confusion that swept Japan during and immediately after the Pacific War. It was a time when primary values were being questioned and examined, when young people—despite their inexperience—were groping to discover the truth. I was often ill during those days, for I had been frail since infancy. Perhaps that is why I became so extremely sensitive and why, when I tried to give direct expression to what I felt so deeply, I naturally turned to poetry.

As a result I developed the habit of occasionally entrusting my thoughts and feelings to poetry. Or not so much to poetry as to slight verses that neither rise above my personal circumstances nor transcend the simple function of giving me solace. Because my verse is so private, the mere thought of presenting it to the public and thus exposing myself to embarrassment is a source of discomfort. Nevertheless, some time ago I allowed a number of poems (far from masterpieces) to appear in periodicals with the hope that they might directly convey what I thought on particular occasions and what I felt about certain topics.

Recently, moreover, I received a request from the Book Division of the *Yomiuri* Newspaper to issue a number of my published poems under a single cover. I felt rather hesitant about giving permission to make my verse widely available to the reading public because it seemed awkward to hand such trivia to posterity. Frankly, I was quite perplexed. But the persistence of the *Yomiuri* people ultimately moved me to yield and give consent. Prior to their request I had published a private, limited edition of verse titled *New Life*, in which I included several short, casual pieces culled from my diaries. With the exception of a few poems transcribed in notebooks as a youth, however, everything that appears in the *Yomiuri* collection has been written since that private collection.

From the viewpoint of a literary critic, my verse may be unworthy of comment. But then I do not write for the critic. My sole intentions are to express forthrightly the feelings that come to me in the context of my daily life and activities, and to convey my hopes for the future. It may sound radical, but I wonder if poetry is not the free expression of such feelings and hopes? The poetry of the *Manyoshu* has survived over a thousand years and continues to throb with life; Whitman's *Leaves of Grass* continues to transcend national boundaries as it powerfully exalts the cries of the individual. In both cases the poetry is alive and meaningful today because it reveals the human spirit and relates to what is basically human—to that which cannot be captured merely by the pedantry of poetic form and convention.

It may seem presumptuous to mention great works like the *Manyoshu* and *Leaves of Grass* in the same breath as amateurish verse. But my purpose in bringing these masterpieces into the discussion is to suggest the direction which I hope the reader's evaluation might take. I would be happy if people see that my feelings resonate more directly with the relatively free and democratic verse of the *Manyoshu* (mid-eighth century) than with the disciplined and aristocratic *waka* of the *Kokinshu* (early tenth century), more with Walt Whitman than with John Keats.

One lamentable result of our advanced modern civilization is the increasing sterility of man's internal world. I know of no greater joy therefore than to imagine that even one line or one phrase of my verse might somehow touch the reader's heart and awaken him to life by indicating what to strive for and how to live. In our turbulent age one needs goals to keep from being swept away by change and upheaval. I fervently hope in my own case that I might always have time to think about the meaning of life, to converse eloquently with nature, and to be sufficiently composed to respond to poetic inspiration.

I would like to express my gratitude to Messrs. Nobuchika Ninomiya and Nobuo Matsuda of the *Yomiuri* Newspaper for their dedicated efforts in seeing the Japanese edition through publication.

November 6, 1971

DAISAKU IKEDA

POSTSCRIPT TO ENGLISH EDITION

I want to convey my deepest appreciation to Dr. Robert Epp, assistant professor in the Department of Oriental Languages at UCLA, for his untiring efforts in the English translation of the works which appear in this volume.

HOPES AND DREAMS

Up from the Soil

Traveler,
Where have you come from?
Where are you going?

I forge ahead
Searching for light
In this unformed moment near dawn,
After the moon has set
But before the sunrise.

I spring up from the soil
To drive the darkness from my mind,
To find a tall tree no storm can bend.

The Crisp Day We Parted

At that crisp moment of parting,
Wind crackled over the plateau;
Waves of pampas grass rippled white,
Flickering the evergreen memories of those days
Since that summer we shared –

One instant in our flash of life,
Under the cryptomerias
On the shores of the Inland Sea –
Like meeting a friendly face
In the window of a passing train.

Once our hearts opened to each other –
Innermost heart to innermost heart –
Such transparent purity,
Lucid as the glitter of the autumn sky,
Is my life's greatest joy.

Even if our eyes should never again meet
As on that crisp day we parted,
I shall believe through the eternity of each moment
In the reality of heart calling to heart,
A reality
    etched forever in my memory.

On that crisp evening when we parted,
Moonlight bound our hearts together
And cast a shadow as a parting gift
Over the winecup we shared as friends.
Autumn winds now sweep across that plateau.

Scattered Blossoms

Cherry trees survive war's ravages,
The sky – pure blue –
    a tumult of falling petals.

Against the backdrop of a world in ruins
People in misery see no blossoms.

Beyond their drifting – how bitter a road
For parent
    for child!

Among the crowded populace, cherry trees bloom,
Their petals stained the color of dawn.

The scene stands, a symbol of our times:
Among men of power
    a few men of peace.

Someone once wrote:
Falling cherry blossoms!
Those still on branches
Will soon fall too.

Millions of blossoms in their springtime:
Why do they fall
    and fall?

Deep in the south seas: O never-to-bloom tree,
Your branches ache beneath the promise of buds.

Already scarred in mind –
in thought –
Your friends that survive
may one day be scattered too.

Will they one day fall and scatter,
never even knowing
Whether everything is transitory
or eternal?

Fallen petals –
petals in bloom –
keep on blooming
Forever
through warm spring days,
through storms!

Pampas Grass

Thatched houses here and there
Beyond the bamboo grove –

Does someone play a lute?
It echoes high and low;

A single stiff stalk listens silently.

The prince who died for the realm,
His princess pining for her lost love –
Have they come from the land of the dead
In the form of pampas fronds?

Alone
    prince and princess
Would miss their court.
Do they head a train of retainers
Arrayed in ample fringes?

Pampas grass
Never grows in boisterous cities.
Has it donned green skirts
And leisurely rooted itself in the hills
Because it wearied of wandering the plains?

Pampas spears!
Whom do you summon so artlessly
With your wiry legs,
With those silvered arms
And golden faces?
Would you tug at the shrouds of the dead?

Breezes sweep the path of fortune.
The flowering pampas sheds tears of dew
Straining against icy winds.

Even dreams of viewing the moon make me forlorn,
Like the picture of harvest moon I saw
As a child.

How did *Manyoshu* poets treat such feelings?
How did *Kokinshu* poets write of them?

At dusk on the Hakone road
Snow-capped Fuji
Soars faintly over the horizon.

Without pampas fields
For the artist's brush to transfer to lacquerware
In delicate gold and silver designs,
That talent would have gone
To waste.

The path of fortune lies under autumn wind.

Pampas grass!
Do you secretly pity the feelings of the aged?
Standing dignified on roadsides
    on embankments,
Do you pass your days ignoring the paths of youth
Or do you gaze wistfully at their dynamic creativity?

Mt. Fuji and I

This poet writes
Of Fuji's splendid harmonies.

Fuji, forgive my endless, my senseless tears
As I gaze at you tonight.

This tear-filled poet with only glints of skill
Lifts his eyes to the heights of his land.

The day is clear, dreams fill the vacant skies;
Clouds well up and hug the mountain.

Fuji burns deep within my being — the object of my love
And Nature's work of art, changeless and ever-changing.

Bokusui solemnly composed those endless songs,
His dialogue with Fuji a challenge to his being.

Clear Fuji, shining Fuji,
Snow-capped Fuji, towering Fuji;

Serene Fuji, Fuji under thunderclouds,
Fuji with sandy skin, with milk-white splendor;

Fuji at daybreak, cloud-shrouded Fuji,
Fuji on a crisp morning, Fuji at night;

Fuji in a gloomy sky, Fuji outstretched,
White-caped in spring, bare in autumn –

Singing to the skies in admiration, I see Fuji
As the acme of goodness, of justice, of the Way.

Snow

To our young girls

It is snowing.
A poet once wrote that snow
Brings messages from heaven.

Fluttering its white garb,
Snow lulls our minds into creamy sleep
And swirls itself into dazzling beauty.
Snowflakes are stiff crystals
That dance through sky like supple petals
To turn the world into poetry.

Its meek appeals unheeded,
Snow continues to cover earth's disguises.
It falls noiselessly,
Brimming like an unstained virgin
With soft smiles and prim looks.

Falling in a hushed chorale,
Snow is the grand harmony of Nature—
A perfectly colorless painting.

Snow is a cold envoy
    who quietly visits the barren winter;
Snow is a silver monarch
    who rules the endless prairie.

I think of snow as a pure melody,
A stunning aria that warms the heart
And drenches the mind.

Snow is an exquisite powder,
A white phantom which again and again
Heaps youthful and palatial dreams
On fields without a hint of the dawn.

Snow touches us with its willingness
To wrap our impurities for a moment
In whiteness
Until spring greens again.

When I see snow's unbounded dialogue,
When I see how well it expresses itself,
I find myself dreaming
Of new possibilities for the world.

Night

A mountain stream,
An evening breeze,
The sound of wind chimes . . .

Night solemnly envelops the forest
As it listens to life's song
Flow from beyond the bell tower.

Swallowed in an abyss of silence,
Vibrant life sleeps fast.

History itself rests in the hush,
Folding its battle wings into the stillness
Where wells of vitality
Will charge them once again with flight.

All things surrender to the night
And slumber peacefully.
Till gold glows through the draped sky,
Till hosts of plants open their green eyes,
Let creation take a deep breath
And sleep off the wish to rest.

The Sea in May

The fiery sun sinks,
Majestically dropping the curtain on another day.

The last glint of the stage burns gold;
The line between sky and sea blurs.
A young man stands like an iris in May's wind,
Gazing into the half-sunk sun
As sea breezes rumple his hair.

I wonder what's on his mind?
Does he ponder his philosophy
And how he hopes to spend his life?
Does he chat with a friend in a far-off land?
Does he stand in sea's roar,
Near where white waves crumble,
In search of strength to meet the dawn?
Does he wait to talk with his lover
On that atoll beyond his sight?

A single sail bobs silently
On the flaming sea.

Autumn Flame

Basking cooly in sunlight,
A scarlet maple leaf
Washes its face in the mountain stream
And offers elegant greetings
To its green companions.

Time

Time –
No color
    no fragrance
No form
    no sound
Moving relentlessly and endlessly on
Time keeps his place.

Time is wordless –
An eternity in a moment, a moment in an eternity:
No momentary pause
    no sentiment
No distance
    no theories.

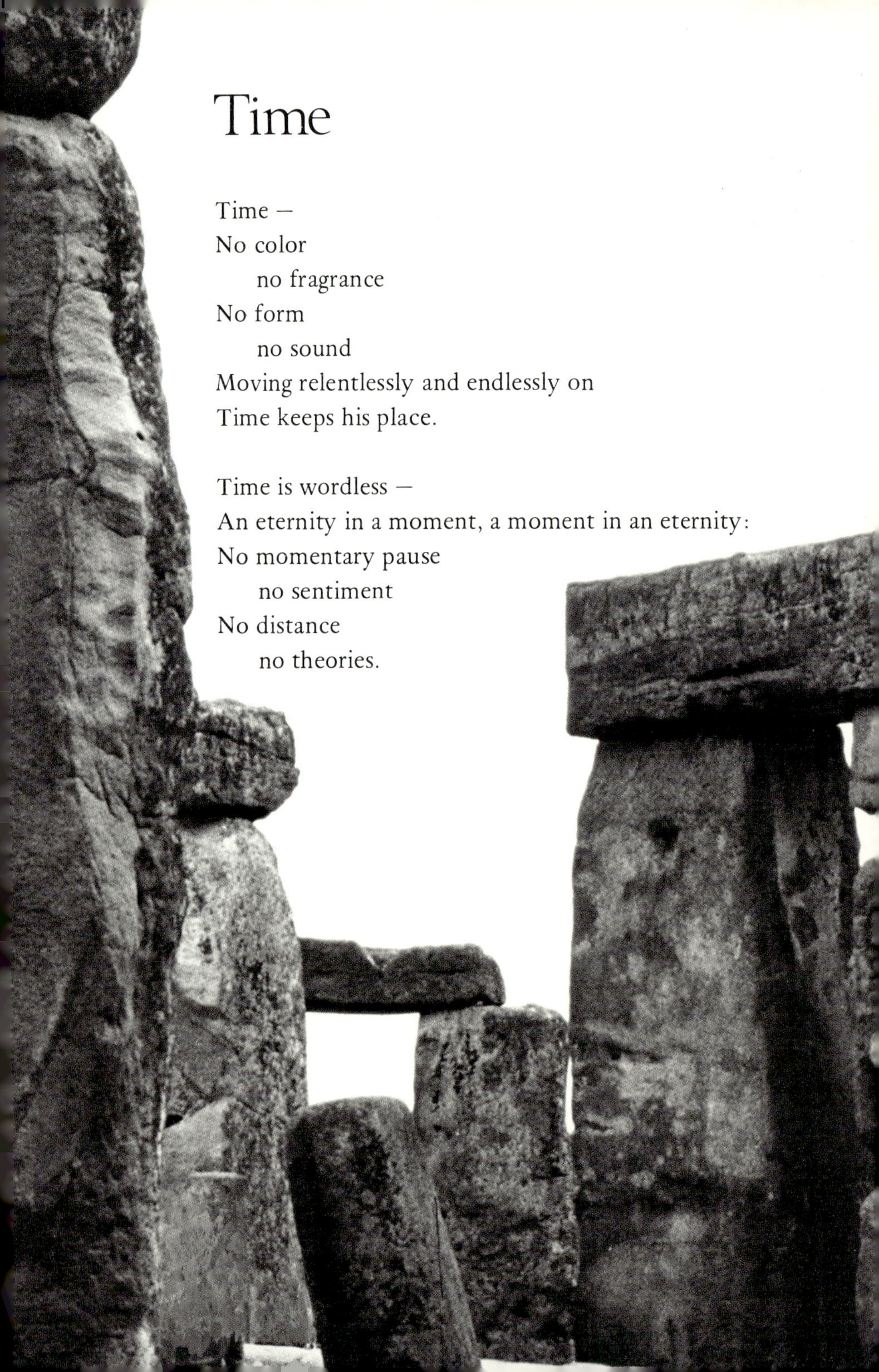

Neither the greatest nor the least
Time flows on
    enfolding the universe
Ignoring man.

Times of anger
    times of fear
Times of joy
    times of hardship
Times of heaviness
    times of emptiness
Times of callousness
    times of tenderness.

Indifferent to the extremes
Of puny human lives,
Time gazes from his vantage point,
Carrying out his tasks with huge strides,
With a glassy, expressionless hush.

Time the ruler –
He is self-assertive,
He has no modesty,
Nothing is as splendidly well defined as he.
He moves on expressionless as a *Noh* mask,
Certain to resolve and resorb
Every affair.

All the while
    the sky has
Bolts of rage for the discouraged,
Bright golden rays for the joyful,
Crystal moons for the weary.

He who in a moment
Confounds man's fondest hopes
And reverses social currents –
Who is he
Who does these wondrous, these silent deeds?
He is Time, the absolute despot.

Not one haughty ruler
Fails to give him homage;
Even swaggering days of glory
Become a paperscrap beneath his gaze.
Mockingly serene,
Time deals the *coup de grace*
To the greedy strategems of petty men.

Time is changeless –
An ancient philosopher in the Orient
Once sought to discover eternal life
And applied his genius to the nature of Time.
He found an element of absolute changelessness
In Time's eternal flux.

This philosopher reasoned
That though Time may indeed be a despot,
If only we knew his essence,
Natural laws allow the possibility
Of making him mankind's mighty ally.

He is mighty who knows the laws of Time.
One who grasps the nature of Time
Commands the greatest honor;
He who knows the law of karma,
Which encompasses Time,
Will accurately assess the present and the future –
No longer misled by the world of things.

Time flows.
He flows
    changingly changeless;
He flows
    infinitely finite.
Pressing on with his macroscopic view,
Time puts both assumption and presumption
Into the categories of a bold metaphysic.
But only those who lay hold of his meaning
Stand forever with Time
At history's end.

Title

Each work has a title;
Echoes of joy and sorrow mingle alternately
In it.
A matchless masterpiece emerges
When the title
Is perfectly portrayed on canvas.

Life also has titles.
As each person discovers his title,
A splendid drama emerges
When title and actor merge.

What this means for life
Is that it may take concerted effort
To sketch a fresh portrait of yourself
On the blank paper of each moment, of the future –
The way a novelist writes,
Laboring to follow his plot;
The way a painter wields his brush,
Laboring with singleness of mind.

The Life of a Literary Giant: Dostoevski

    Rebel against God
    Genius at opposition
    Proponent of the national spirit
    Revealer of the distant future –
Countless epithets have been hurled at him.

Constantly criticized
    constantly praised,
Ever himself,
Unwavering if gloomy,

Banished to Siberia,
His noble youth deranged by blizzards,
Driven by tenacious rage
Through the short arctic nights of Petersburg,
An eventful life afflicted by sickness
Distressed by poverty –

For all that, never yielding,
No matter how desperate life's struggle,
He turned each battle into precious cement
To build a glowing and radiant world
Which never stopped firing his mind.

He never pursued art for art's sake,
Never pursued the salon's aristrocratic charms,
Never took the leisure to indulge in sentiment.
Dunned by time and debtors,
He merely wrote in search of something
    to procure the morrow's bread
    to liquidate his endless debts.
No time to spare for polishing diction,
Moved by endless passion he simply waits and waits
As though gliding through air.

He emerged from the tattered greatcoats of the masses
And sank quietly into increasing fulfillment
Where he gave his whole being to the very heart of life.
Swamped with the filth and the stench and the tumult
Of the sick
    the criminal
        the destitute
His afterglow steadily stirs the age that followed him
As he fades inexorably away.

Genius

The world a genius depicts is always spectacular:
    A display of miracles,
    The overturning of common sense,
    Unlimited creativity.
Anyone reeling in the vivid, uncharted future of the genius
Will wildly cheer him on.

The world a genius occupies is always a lightning bolt:
    A revelation of inspiration,
    The certainty of conviction,
    Instantaneous action.
Anyone confused by the incredible quickness of the genius
Will be dazzled and breathless.

The world within the genius is always tragic:
    The agony of madness,
    The fear of being backed against a wall,
    The grief of exile.
Anyone terror-stricken by the poetic fate of the genius
Will take comfort in his own simple life.

The world the genius seeks may be simple after all:
    The concord of stability,
    The humming of happiness,
    Tunes of tranquility.
Anyone who notes his simple hopes
Will naturally feel affection for the genius.

But some geniuses have yet to appear among us:
    Geniuses of humanism,
    Geniuses at creating happiness.
As far as I am able,
I would take up the gauntlet for humanism
Led by a great Life master clothed in compassion
And the laws of the macrocosm.

Travelers

Travelers pass,
Searching today and tomorrow
For new roads to happiness.

I cannot know their hearts;
Perhaps they are loaded with grief,
Perhaps they are lightened with joy.

Merely to survive the chill of dawn
Or the heat of evening,
These travelers are forever on the move;
Though buffeted, they hold to the road.

Where do these countless travelers
Come from, you ask, where do they go?
They come from sojourns with tragedy
To seek out paths of hope.

The poet Wakayama Bokusui writes,
> "How many hills and rivers must we cross
> To reach a land without loneliness?
> We set out again today . . ."

The people of such a land
Have dreams,
Gardens which joy can flower in,
Arenas for democracy,
Unerring ideals,
A stage for all to act upon.

Travelers, advance and I shall follow
On Man's endless trek
From paths of wrath to paths of joy.

Dreams

This morning I dreamed
Of something pleasant beyond words.
But when I awoke
It faded instantly away.

My dream of being chased by something dreadful
Yesterday
Continues to haunt my mind.

Even with no one to influence it,
Ku's fitful whirl fills my mind.

A solemnly unnatural whirl constantly reappears
On that line between reality and illusion
Deep in the mist-shrouded hills and fields,
Haunting now a stranger, now a friend.

In life after death,
We sense joy and anger, sadness and pleasure,
In the same space we felt them before death;
We shall wander through that reality
Where life and death are one.

If I must dream,
I would dream
    wonders.

Treasures

Okura Yamanoue wrote in the *Manyoshu*;
"Gold and silver and jewels
Amount to nothing;
The greatest treasure is a child."

My greatest treasure is health,
Together with the sparkling hope to be creative
And to live my ideals.

I also treasure
A young man's glistening eyes,
The teenager's soiled overalls,
The farmer's gnarled hands,
A grandmother's selfless wrinkles,
melting into smiles.

These people live affirmatively:
Fulfilling themselves,
Glowing with fresh fascination for life.

As I think of them, I find myself thrilling
To a new treasure.

Believer

In Nature, a recurring circle of seasons;
On the globe, a precise twenty-four hour rotation;
Everything
Following tracks by eternal cosmic law.

What about the macrocosm of the individual?

Kant saw it as
"The starry heavens above me, the moral law within."

What of me . . . ?

Meshing the inner dimensions of my life
With the flow of the limitless universe,
I move in concert with distant tracks;
I have made those ultimate laws
Objects of my private faith.

Returning home after a day crowded with activities,
I gaze at stars glittering across the skies
And confirm the laws deep within me.

And,
Enraged by the world's tragedies and injustices,
I resolve once more
To be a dedicated pioneer,
Opening paths for men on the journey
Through birth, old age, sickness and death.

Angels of Peace

Angels of peace, you bearers of culture!
Ah, the fervent breath
Of my friends on fife and drum –
You fashion a single ever-fresh flower
Dressing up our dreary world.

Marching to the flanks, or forward, or pinwheeling
At the drum major's bidding,
The elegance of close-order drill
Creates a divinely fluid dance flowing from the fervor
That charges your minds, charges your bodies.

Along the chilly paths of discipline
In our chaotic and jaded age,
Your radiant circle (a ring of life linked with precious life)
Emits the sparkling good sense of youth
And a well-wrought song of triumph.

Daughters of the nameless masses,
Pioneers in smashing the walls between people
As you melt the seasoned ices of ideology,
You are the unofficial envoys –
True and trustworthy angels of peace.

Strangers to political craft,
Strangers to diplomatic strategems,
Without speaking a word, you spread our philosophy of peace,
You extend the frontiers of friendship –
Touching the people where they are.

Using neither bullets nor bayonets,
But only simple fifes and drums,
You play the basic rhythms of the Mystic Universe;
None can help responding from deep within.
Certainly you shall spur the world to peace!

Yes, we find in you a florid oasis
Greening our spiritual desert:
Your light-hearted "Do Re Me,"
Your lyrical and lucid "Moonlight above the Castle Ruins,"
Your "Symphony of Joy."

I shall never forget
Tears gleaming in the eyes of those angels
Who see from afar the bulwarks of world solidarity
Beyond the soaring horizon.
I cheer the tunes in every glistening pearly tear.

As you evade the flames of war,
Clearing the din of progress
And announcing to all the New Truth,
You light now one, now another
Light of life among us.

The lights you've lit merge into patterns
Spreading everywhere over the gloom,
Over the ugliness of these latter days;
Your light soon will generate the passion
To fire all our tomorrows.

My Friends Behind the Scenes

Oh my so proud young friends –
On this hushed morning
You face the dawn carrying the news of our *Kosen-rufu* –
Today
    Tomorrow
Acting like Tathagata's messengers,
You are the true pioneers of the people.

You – not those honored in the footlights,
But you who work behind the scenery –
I'll never forget what you've done,
Having myself once played the same role.

The English won
The fierce battle of Waterloo,
And the French were routed,
But Victor Hugo cried,
"Who was the real victor?"

It was the unheralded commander Carbronne
Who cried *"Merde!"* in the face of the allied cannon,
Fighting bravely on,
Refusing to surrender until he was routed.

Those who sang the true triumphal song of victory
Were neither generals nor officers,
But those brave souls in the rank and file,
The tenacious privates.

Those who create and influence history
Are not the heroes;
The heroes are those who stake their lives behind the scenes.
It is the same in propagating our movement.
I put my hopes in you alone;
You who sustain us are the motors for Kosen-rufu.

I salute you all.
Eventually the whole world will accept you
As those having made the greatest contribution
In laying the foundation for propagating the Mystic Law.

Hope

In every land
Boys burning with hope
Study hard.
A valued flower will bloom
In every home
    in every nation
When each boy
Matures.

In it is the same
In England,
In America
Or China,
In the Soviet Union
And France.

A good tree
    must certainly come from
A good seedling.
A beautiful flower
    must certainly have once been
A beautiful bud.

Thus a fine boy
Will surely become a fine young man.
A fine young man
    can surely become
A fine member of society.
A boy burning with hope
And moving ahead
    can surely become
A fine leader.

Then burn with hope,
Standing stubbornly against every blizzard;
Burn with hope and study hard.

Climb that mountain!
Ford that river!
Hope is charged with courage.

You may be poor at math.
You may be poor at science.
But persist until you master them all,
For each is an aspect of the cosmic law.

Hope
Emerges from striving,
For hope
Is pregnant with happiness and peace.

Hope gives life a dream.
Life without dreams is dreary.
He who holds forever to
    youthful hopes
Will be a fine adult –
Neither calculating nor interested in himself alone,
Nor yet concerned with fame.

You must study tenaciously
Now while you are young
To attain happiness and peace.

Young Boys

Ah, glittering like future knights,
My young friends gallop through the wild
From beyond distant visions:
Bright lads, leaping furiously in the golden wind,
Mighty young messengers from the future
Dashing toward that new city.

Minds – impressionable as ripened fruit;
Minds – sensitive as thermometers,
Taking everything in,
Your lives at sunrise, despising injustice.
You see rainbows of hope
Hanging above the wavecaps;
You hear light's throb beat rhythmically
Even on a single leaf.

Boys!
Boys!
Respond to the whole of life
With the potent and passionate throb of your souls.
Grow persistently straight,
Piercing sharply into the sky
Like lively green bamboo.

You are uncompleted carvings.
Soon you will gallantly appear
On life's stage,
Latent actors molding every freedom.
You must record wholeheartedly,
Day by day,
On receptive blank canvases,
The golden letters appropriate to youth.

You cried to pure clouds adrift in the summer blue.
Your voices will continue to echo
Forever through space;

And on some future night those warm hopes
Sent to constellations from a frigid night
Will congeal and glitter through the sky.

Boys!
Let ideas impressed on your minds
During youth
Flow forever through your lives like water.
The heart of this Truth you have finally grasped
Will surely glow like an undying beacon
While throwing clear beams over seas of gloom.

Boys!
All you boys,
The day draws near when you will launch into the waves.
Life's seas are rough,
But those stars burning fiercely in every breast,
Your flaming ideals, will never wane.

No, you cannot avoid one day
Being touched by the world's brutality;
Your unsoiled lives will also
Know the taste of grief.
But boys,
All you boys –
No matter how oppressed you feel,
No matter what trials of adulthood
Might darken your unshaven cheeks,
Never let your hearts be downcast.

Boys, you are
Princes of a world with unlimited potential!
Though confronted by towering cliffs,
Never console yourselves with indulgent words like
"That's too much for me." Though vexed to tears,
Stand alone and challenge reality to the very limit
With every ounce of strength you can summon.

Be buffeted by waves,
Scale steep cliffs,
Sweat in the sweltering heat,
Clear thorns from your chosen path
With that restless youthful tenacity!

Your eyes are windows to innocent lives.
Never cloud those mirrors of crystal minds
By debasing them with perversions of your talent;
Rather forge ahead undaunted,
Boldly confronting society and its endless flux.

Even a phoenix was once a chick.
But when the flap of its wings fills the sky,
Surely its day of hardships will be transformed
And it will shriek lusty songs of victory,
Bursting with joy over the triumph of all mankind.

Boys – the future of mankind!
The world's destiny has been entrusted
To your hearts, to your hands:
Our small society your playground,
The near future your possession!
I truly hope you prosper
On the road ahead.

Notes on the Poems

page 16 UP FROM THE SOIL

At the age of nineteen, Daisaku Ikeda attended his first Nichiren Shoshu discussion meeting, which was led by then President Josei Toda. Immediately, he sensed that he had found a master and a philosophy to live by. He expressed his feelings by standing up and reciting this impromptu poem entitled "*Jiyu*." Everyone present was astonished that he had used this unusual word, since *Jiyu-no Bosatsu* is the Buddhist term for people in ordinary society who feel a mission to help others.

page 18 THE CRISP DAY WE PARTED

During World War II, the youthful Ikeda was forced to stay at home because of ill health. He composed this poem as he watched his friends leave for the front.

page 20 SCATTERED BLOSSOMS

Toward the close of the war, President Ikeda's elder brother was killed in action in Southeast Asia, and he wrote this poem to his brother's memory.

Stanza 6
"Someone once wrote . . . ": After the war, President Ikeda had discovered this anonymous poem on the wall of a fire-gutted house in Tokyo.

page 24 PAMPAS GRASS

Stanza 10
"*Manyoshu*": "Collection of Ten Thousand Leaves", a collection (c.759) of 4,500 poems from the seventh century and even earlier. The *Manyoshu*

poems are characterized by their simple freshness and sincerity of feeling. "*Kokinshu*": a collection of later verse (c.905). The *Kokinshu* poems are more concerned with formality and perfection of language than originality of feeling.

Stanza 11
"Hakone road": the road between Tokyo and the resort area of Hakone and a popular subject in both art and literature which evokes feelings of melancholy.

page 28 MT. FUJI AND I

Since ancient times, Mt. Fuji has stirred the soul of the Japanese people as a symbol of grandeur and lofty purpose. The Nichiren Shoshu head temple, Daisekiji, lies at its foot, and so Mt. Fuji has a special significance for Soka Gakkai members.

Stanza 6
"Bokusui": early twentieth century naturalist poet.

page 40 TIME

Stanza 6
"*Noh* mask": *Noh* is the most important form of Japanese drama and took its present form in the fourteenth century. It is a perfected harmony of dance, poetry, music, mime and acting. The main character wears a formalized mask, while the other characters wear mask-like make-up.

page 52 DREAMS

Stanza 3
"*Ku*'s fitful whirl": *Ku* is a Buddhist concept which describes a state of neither being nor non-being.

page 56 ANGELS OF PEACE

This poem was written to the *Kotekitai,* the girls' fife and drum corps of the Soka Gakkai. President Ikeda initiated the *Kotekitai* as well as the Brass Band for young men in 1956. They perform worldwide in parades and culture festivals.

Stanza 7
"Moonlight over the Castle Ruins": *"Kojyo no Tsuki"*, a popular Japanese song which is a favorite of President Ikeda.

page 60 MY FRIENDS BEHIND THE SCENES

This poem was written to the newsboys who deliver the *Seikyo Shimbun,* the daily newspaper of the Soka Gakkai.

Stanza 1
"the news of our *Kosen-rufu*": *Kosen-rufu* means world peace through individual happiness, which is the ultimate goal of Nichiren Shoshu.

"Tathagata's messengers": Tathagata, or *Nyorai* in Japanese, is one of the titles of the Buddha. In particular, the name symbolizes the essential Buddha nature inherent within each individual.

About the Author

Daisaku Ikeda is President of the 15-million member Soka Gakkai International organization. He is a prolific writer, having written over fifty books and hundreds of essays and poems. His popular appeal has made him one of the most widely-read authors in Japan today.

Mr. Ikeda was born in Tokyo in 1928 and experienced severe hardships growing up in a nation torn apart by war. In 1947, he joined Nichiren Shoshu and began studying under his master, Josei Toda, the Soka Gakkai's second president. The following year, he graduated from the Toyo Business School and entered Fuji Junior College, where he earned a degree in economics.

He became the editor of the *Seikyo Shimbun,* a Soka Gakkai publication which has followed the meteoric growth of the organization and is currently the fifth largest daily in the world. In 1960, he was inaugurated as the society's third president, becoming the spiritual leader of the Soka Gakkai's members in over eighty nations.

Mr. Ikeda has traveled extensively in the interest of world peace and has met with international leaders as well as ordinary people everywhere. He is the founder of Soka University and several secondary schools throughout Japan, and has initiated many cultural and educational exchange programs among universities around the world. In 1975, he was awarded an honorary doctoral degree from Moscow State University.

Photo Credits
pages 40-41 by Harold M. Lambert
pages 42-43 by Ewing Galloway